I AM not coming out today, thank you all the same for asking. I didn't go out yesterday or the day before yesterday, and I'm sure I won't be coming out tomorrow or the day after tomorrow.

Because it is not safe, that's why. Thanks to you people.

If I were foolish enough to come out from behind this big, strong door, I'd find myself plunged headlong into a battle for survival.

Take the garden, for a start. Surely a peaceloving, easy-going fella like me is entitled to think of the garden as a place of tranquillity and safety.

Not on your life! Not the way that outsized, overfed (and over-rated) Siamese cat from next door creeps up on me. Why you people keep cats —!

Take a simple pleasure like trotting along to the local butcher's shop to scrounge, snitch or steal the odd bone or a few pounds of best steak.

It's just not on, not these days!

For a start, the street is full of noisy fast cars filled with drivers who just love to blow horns loudly. To say nothing of millions of people who edge me off the pavement.

And butchers' shops aren't what they used to be. I blame it all on the "progress" you people are so mad on. Shop doors shut, meat kept covered (and some even pre-packed — oh, ugh!) and butchers who have been brainwashed (doubtless by cat-loving hygienic fanatics) into thinking dogs should be barred from their shops.

And lastly, but by no means least, there's that dreadful French poodle three doors away. The way you people drool over her — really! As soon as she sees me, she's in our garden without as much as by your leave, yapping away about why don't we get to know each other better.

I'll stay here, thank you. I know when I'm well off. I'm only sticking my head out because I'm very keen on fresh air and exercise.

Well, I've had at least half a dozen deep breaths of outside air. Enough is enough! Now back to the nearest armchair for a rest from such exertions!

£1.95

WAIT till she comes in and sees me with this ferocious, deadly-dangerous ball of wool! She'll do her nut!

"Oh you cheeky-boy!" she'll say. "Leave Mumsy's wool alone!"

That's what I get all the time. If you'll pardon my mixed metaphor (whatever that is), as a cat I live a dog's life.

"Oh you cheeky boy!" she yells. "Come down from that pantry shelf at once."

(Why leave luscious steak lying around on an open plate anyway? It's also unhygienic!)

"Oh you cheeky boy!" she lets fly. "Get off Mumsy's bed!"

(She wasn't even in it, so why object to my using it for a quiet snooze? Beds for her and him and all the noisy kids . . . but none for me.)

And that's how it goes all day long. I do what I can . . . and she does her nut.

And then **he** comes home. (He skips out every morning and disappears all day. He only comes back because there's a meal ready. At least that's what I think!) Before I know where I am, we start all over again.

"Come on, you brute, get out of my chair!" he says.

His chair indeed! Who does he think uses it all day when he's out gallivanting wherever it is people go to gallivant?

It all goes to show what sweet forbearing creatures we cats are. We let people live in our nice cosy homes, put up with all the clatter-clatter, bang-bang, whine-whine (oh, those vacuums!) and yakkitty-yak!

Not only do we get no thanks — people won't even show us how to open doors, milk-bottle tops, or tins of cat food!

Oh — oh, I can hear her doing her nut again in the kitchen. Why do I keep forgetting Mumsy doesn't like dead mice?

OCCUPATIONAL HAZARDS
Are you kidding?
I've only five left out of my nine!

MOTTO
Ginger them up!

JUST the other day, I was happily snuffling my way along the street from my usual stop-and-sniff spot to my next stop-and-sniff spot. Like I say, I was happy. I hadn't a care in the world, apart from the usual ones I always have. Like "When is the next meal coming?"

Then I saw It. And It was one of you people!

Mind you, I wasn't too sure at first. It could have passed for one of us walking around on hindlegs. Then I saw the leather jacket and jeans and I knew It couldn't be one of us. I'm not slow on the uptake, you understand.

Now I know how smart and attractive we are with our long hair — and particularly with the super-duper overhanging fringe style around the eyes. But *must* you people copy us?

It looked just sloppy! I felt quite heartbroken at the thought of what would happen if all you people started to copy It.

Hairdressers would be out of work, shampoo manufacturers would be forced to expand and work overtime, and opticians would do booming business cutting eyelets in your ringlets, if you follow me.

So let me say briefly — get your hair cut, you scruffy lot!

You people might think that I am being unreasonable. But I'm not. If the good Lord had intended you people to look as beautiful as the likes of me, you people would have been born not only with long hair all over your eyes, but with your own personal fur coats as well, to say nothing of a first-class nose. And you people would have been born intelligent enough to walk on all fours.

So please — let's cut out this long hair lark. I will put it no stronger. I will issue no threats . . . except to add darkly that if you people persist in copying us, you might well find survival to be a case of "Hair Today, Gone Tomorrow."

You have been warned!

"A WORD in your ear, friend," he says in a voice that's too full of menace to be ignored.

So I sit — and listen.

"There's going to be a few changes around here," he says. "Starting from now! Henceforth, friend, you'll do a lot more giving and a lot less taking.

"Like giving me first crack at my own meals. Like keeping out of my basket when I'm in it. Like making room for me at the fireside when I wish to indulge myself in a snooze.

"I further wish to inform you, friend," he goes on, "that all this crummy propaganda you have been spreading to the effect that we dogs are stupid, bone-idle, canine nitwits is not only untrue but also downright false."

"Floppy-ears," I say pleadingly, "how can you say such things . . . ?"

"And that's another thing, friend, he barks in my ear. "My name is not Floppy-ears, as you very well know. My name is Sir . . . my full name is Sir Cecil of Tare, but you may just call me Sir. Understand?"

"Yes, sir," I say weakly.

"Right, friend." He nods — and gives me a heave to the back door. "It's your day to patrol the garden and keep the birds off the fruit. Get to work! And don't be noisy when you come in — I shall be sleeping."

"Yes, sir," I say.

Something tells me that something awful has happened to me. I think I might even run away — leave home — wander the face of the earth. I'll bet that would make old Floppy-ears — sorry. Sir Old Floppy-ears! — cry his beady eyes out!

Or would it? On second thoughts, I think I'll stick around here and just suffer like the noble martyr I am.

TAILPIECE
Whoever said "Share and share alike" must have been a bullying dog in his day!

OCCUPATIONAL HAZARDS
Wire — bars and bars of it!
Having to bathe in public.
Draughts.
Other birds. Rough creatures.
Sneaky hungry cats.

MOTTO
Watch the birdie.

W E especially like people who let us out of our cage. Do you blame us? How would YOU like to be cooped up day in, day out, in a small wire bin?

We also like people who talk. We talk ourselves, you know. And that's more than you can say about all the cats, dogs and what-have-you pets you care to name!

But even though we can have a chat with you now and again, life isn't exactly rosy for us.

We spend so much time preening ourselves in the mirror, buffing our beaks till they shine, and practising the most flirtatious attitudes — and for what?

For someone to poke at us with their finger and cluck, "Kiss for Joey!" It's insulting, that's what it is!

And does anybody ever teach us the latest top twenty hit? Oh, no! Silly little nursery jingles — that's all we get.

Ah well, we mustn't grumble too much — or someone will throw a dark cloth over our cage to keep us quiet. But at least we'd have some privacy . . .

Mind you, it's not a bad life. We are pampered really. Plenty to eat, lots to drink, a well-furnished cage, and allowed out now and again for a flutter.

You can't have everything, can you?

WHO said "Yappy little things!" — who dared even to whisper it? Step forward and let's have you!

I'll have you know that the wise man who went on record as saying good things come in small packets probably owned a dog just like me.

The good Lord made dogs for all kinds of purposes. Hunting dogs, tracking dogs, show dogs, beautiful dogs.

And we were chosen to be the small, sturdy independent home-loving dogs. To help us, we were given an outsize dash of courage, an unswerving sense of loyalty, an overdose of love and affection, and an impish sense of humour — the whole mixture being knitted together with an inbuilt appreciation of the good things in life. Such as warm fires, cosy armchairs, comfortable beds, good food, and regular playtimes.

We like people . . . but we love homes. Look how generous-hearted we are — we never once object to people sharing our homes with us.

OCCUPATIONAL HAZARDS
Peace-loving neighbours.
High kerbs.
Nervous postmen.
Fast-walking owners.

MOTTO
East is east, but Westie's best!

IT'S not often I ever hear you lot talking good sense, but I would certainly never argue with those of you who say, "If a thing's worth doing, then it's worth doing well!"

That is why I take the subject of sleep so seriously. I can truthfully say that I have devoted much of my time to the study and *practice* of sleep.

You may wonder how one can possibly *study* the subject of sleep. That's because you lot have no imagination. Everywhere I go in our house, I am studying this place and that . . . with a view to sleep.

Is it warm? Draught-proof? Quiet? Out of sight? Is it forbidden? (For some odd reason, I sleep so much better in forbidden places. Particularly on top of newly-ironed clothes, or inside wardrobes and tall-boys.)

Apart from the choice of resting place, I have also to consider carefully, the duration of sleep. Please don't think I just get my head down, shut my eyes, and leave the rest to chance. Oh, dear me no!

I have to calculate how long before the next meal is due, then work out how long I can sleep before putting in an appearance.

Everything I do really revolves around sleep. If I am to chase birds or hunt mice, I always know just how long I can carry out such violent exercise before I need to collapse in a well-chosen place to recuperate.

There's only one thing wrong about sleeping, I find. I do so much of it that it does wear me out. I get so tired.

But then one must make sacrifices, mustn't one? You reckon?

I do, anyway. So excuse me while I rest my eyes, let my brain slow down to idling speed, and just sink into wonderful, wonderful sleep . . .

Zzzzzzzzz!

EXCUSE me laughing, but you people really are a funny lot!

To start with, you live all wrong. You work all day — when you should be resting. And you sleep all night — when you should be out enjoying yourselves.

You work hard to earn to buy expensive furniture, when all you really need is a cosy draught-free spot to lie down in, something soft to lay your head against, and some peace and quiet so that you can sleep undisturbed.

I don't understand all this must-go-to-work lark.

Having settled the question of one's comforts, there remains the question of one's food.

Now frankly I can't see you lot wriggling through the long grass around the compost heap in an effort to catch a field mouse or two. Neither can I imagine you hiding in a flower bed, making like a rose bush, until the right second to pounce on a bird silly enough to come within range.

So your food is quite a problem. If only you — but wait!

It strikes me that *my* food might well become more of a problem than it already is if you lot stopped buying liver and fish and cans of lovely food.

Which means of course I've been rather hasty in suggesting you change your way of life at all.

Indeed, on reflection I am more than convinced that you wonderful lot are really doing a grand job, earning all that lovely lolly with which to buy poor deserving cases like myself more lovely nosh.

So press on — regardless. Regardless of anything you might hear or say or learn to the contrary.

And by the way, if you should happen to be working a little harder and longer and more profitably just now, I would mention that I haven't tasted a rainbow trout or a Scotch salmon in ages . . .

I DON'T know why I should be expected to come along and tell you good people all about us Dalmatians. I mean, it's so unnecessary, isn't it? All you need to know about us is right here in front of your eyes in black and white.

And what do you see? Apart from spots, of course! And please don't harp on about them. Everybody thinks they can make jokes about our spots! Oh, those corny jokes! Names like "Blotter" "Old Inkstains," and so on . . . to suggestions like — "Try bleach — or one of the wash-whiter-than-white powders."

When you look at a Dalmatian you'll see strength of dignity and loyalty. Now what more could you want in a dog?

We're very aristocratic, too. "Carriage trade" dogs we used to be called, from the days when we trotted along behind the carriages of the wealthy nobility. We can trace our line of ancestors 'way, 'way back to the few original Dalmatians brought to Britain by travellers who knew a good thing when they saw it.

Well, that's about all I'm going to say. I feel, to be frank about it, that all this "I'm the dog for you" stuff is wrong.

MOTTO
Always on the spot.

What should be done is for you good people to be telling us dogs just why you think "We're the right people to own you!"

It would be very interesting . . .

Now go on, tell me I'm a trouble-maker, an agitator, and all that. I'm not! But I do have a mind of my own. Ask any Dalmatian owner and you'll be told just how intelligent and deep-thinking we are!

Better still, take the plunge, buy one and find out for yourself!

OCCUPATIONAL HAZARDS
Apart from people who flip white-wash brushes around carelessly or having to sleep in rooms with strongly-striped wallpaper, life for us is no problem at all. So there!

FOR too long, we aristocratic Pekingese have been too good natured to you people. The time has come when the next person to say of any of us "What happened to its face? Someone push it in?" is liable to be thumped.

And the same goes for anyone who grins like an idiot and says, "What is it? A long-haired fossil?"

Accustomed as our honourable ancestors (may they yap in peace!) were to the best things in life such as servants galore, the finest of food, the luxury of royal palaces (to mention but a few!) we Pekingese of today take badly with living with the likes of you.

Stands to reason, doesn't it? None of you ever think of how much we would appreciate a silken cushion on which to snooze . . . none of you seem capable of offering us courtesy and good service. (Or to put it another way, "Would you like to partake of some food now?" is more preferable to "Nosh up! Come and get it!")

Respect for us Pekingese is something we need more of. Too many of you look down on us with ill-concealed contempt and doubtless thinking of great hulking brutes such as Alsatians, Great Danes, and Afghan hounds, mutter epithets like "Lapdog!"

I'll have you know that we Pekes are ready to take on anything or anybody. All we ask is — one at a time, please!

We're tough, ruthless, demanding, and fearless. Whoever said, "Good things come in small packages" was really thinking of us.

Perhaps I have inadvertently given you the impression that I am complaining about you people. Perhaps you are thinking I'm the type who bites the hand that feeds me, so to speak.

How wrong you are! All I am *suggesting*, in the nicest possible way, is that you people make a few changes in our way of living.

If you would move out of these small poky houses you seem to like and dwell in palaces, or even a second-hand baronial hall, if there's nothing else available, it would help us not to feel so shut in.

And if you could tiptoe around instead of hashy-bashy rushing here and there, and bow when you approach us, it would help to make us feel more appreciated.

A few words in Chinese would make us feel our ancient line of ancestors was not being overlooked. Surely you could learn the Chinese for "Walkies" or "Time you went out to the garden for you-know-what"?

A little effort from you people . . . is that too much to ask?

I WAS sleeping that quiet I wasn't even snoring. Then all of a sudden the roof fell on me. I died twice — once from shock, once from lack of breath — and there he was.

Bighead had arrived.

"Here," he says, all sorry for himself, "I'm fed up. Why won't you come out and play?"

If only his weight wasn't crushing my spine, I'd have given him a few crushing answers. But for once I'm· at a disadvantage.

"Go away, please!" I say in a choked whisper.

He settles all the more heavily. "Here," he says, "you don't half make a fine pillow. All fluffy and warm."

He snuggles, snorts and sniffles against my beautiful ice-blue fur. "Smashing!" he says ecstatically. "What I've been missing!"

I try — oh, I really try! — to throw him off. But I can't even clobber him with my tail — he's squashed it.

So I remember what my mamma always told me. "When you can't scratch, spit, struggle or survive any longer, don't give up — give in!"

I jolt Bighead awake with a ripple down my back.

"What about you and me," I purr sweetly, "going out to play games in the garden?"

"Oh, goody-goody!" he drools. "Let's play man and woman and I'll chase you first."

I close my eyes, exhausted at the very thought of running around. He has such a revolting amount of energy.

"Why don't we play hide-and-seek?" I say. "You go and hide. I'll count — oh to a million, and you'll have time then to find a really good hiding place."

He bounds away, slithers across the hall, and out into the garden.

I sigh with relief, take my first real deep breath for hours . . . and quietly go back to sleep.

I THINK I would like people if I knew what people really were. All I really know about is my mother. And I like her even better than a saucer of milk. (Besides who needs a saucer of milk when Mum's around?)

I'm not sure I like being a kitten. Strange objects — ever so huge and high they are — keep swooping down on me with sounds of "Ooh!" and "Ah!" and "He's so *cute!*"

And suddenly I feel myself *flying!* Yes, really! Flying! How else could I get so high off the ground?

It's not much fun being a kitten. You have such a small tummy . . . you no sooner start a meal than you have to finish — or burst. Mummy eats and eats and eats. I wish I was grown-up . . .

I don't really sleep in this basket. I just climbed in to try it for size . . . and to make sure it was empty. I like climbing into things. Especially warm places where you curl up and sleep for ages. (I could sleep longer if I had a bigger tummy and didn't have to wake up to eat.)

I don't like being bossed. And Mummy bosses me all the time. "Wash your face!" . . . "Clean your ears!" . . . "Lick your coat!" . . . "It's time you went outside !"

There's one thing I wanted to ask . . . oh yes! · Tell me what are people? Is there enough liver and fish and milk for them, too? And do they have big tummies?

OCCUPATIONAL HAZARDS
What's that mean?

MOTTO
Food for thought.

TO tell the truth, I'm feeling very unhappy. This may come as a surprise to you people, considering how my cheerful countenance may well have misled you. But unhappy I definitely am!

The truth is that I'm beginning to despair of ever winning a beauty contest. All these years of reading about Cruft's Blue Ribbon this and Champion of Champions that . . . and I've still to get in even as an interested spectator.

Oh, I know why I am never entered. The competition would be so one-sided that other dogs wouldn't have a look-in. At least that is what some people must think.

But I'm not so sure. I'm certainly devastatingly good looking — but I'm not all that sure that I'm over-whelmingly beautiful.

Well, if you will insist, I'll allow myself to be persuaded. So I'm breathtakingly beautiful!

But once again, I become most unhappy, even though I do put a brave and uncomplaining face on things. Because since I am so strikingly beautiful, why, oh why, are film producers, pet food manufacturers, TV directors,

to say nothing of the general mass of you people, not beating a path to my door?

In brooding about the problem, I have (naturally) come up with the only answer.

Jealousy!

You people are so jealous that you are all part of one giant conspiracy to keep me from the fame and fortune I so richly deserve.

There is a great deal I could do to expose your selfish underhand ways, but I shall remain, as always, uncom-plaining. I shall keep my dignity. I shall not demean myself.

But if danger strikes and you need help, don't send for me. Contact Radar, or Rin Tin Tin, or Lassie — or even your next-door neighbour's poodle, for all I care.

I shall be too busy brooding over the punishment of being born so beautiful. In addition, I shall also be doing my throat exercises which will enable me to bark more deeply, more loudly, and more annoyingly than ever.

Oh yes, I can B A R K! People have been know to complain — sorry, I meant to hear me — four streets away!

I'm not *just* a pretty face, you know!

I LIKE folk as much as I like sheep. Ay, I do. Being one of the working classes in the dog world, I'm not one for expecting too much in the way of fancy frills from what life has to offer.

Give me a farmyard to regard as my own, some hills with sheep scattered around, and an owner who knows good work when it's done and doesn't forget to feed me well, and I'm content.

Mind you, I've got feelings that can get ruffled at times.

It hurts, you know, when people glance indifferently at a plain, hard-working dog like me and then drool — ay, drool! — at one of those lapdog ninnies that couldn't tell a sheep from a cow, never mind a ewe from a ram!

You see that long nose of mine? It's super-sensitive — when it comes to sheep. Believe me or not, every time I pass the grocer's in the village my nose quivers . . . and that's merely tinned mutton!

I'll tell you one thing I never, never do. Count sheep when I can't get to sleep!

OCCUPATIONAL HAZARDS
Stupid mothers at the lambing season.
Houseproud farmers' wives and farmyard mud.
Getting woolly-minded in my old age.
Mutton in my dog meat.
Sheepish grins.
Everlasting chorus of "Baas!"

MOTTO
I work, ewe work!

THOUGH I do like people, frankly they do make silly mistakes at times. Take a look at this rotten old grass, for example — who could ever consider eating that all day long?

Anyone with any intelligence would know there's nothing more appealing than a fresh young lettuce. And it's not only food that you people are not very clever about.

There's the business of nicknames . . . I mean, what's all this "Easter Bunny" nonsense. It is nonsense, you know. I mean, why not call us "Christmas Bunnies" or "St Valentine Bunnies" or what?

And the craze is spreading. I've heard talk about Playboy Bunnies and Playmate Bunnies. Really it's enough to make any self-respecting rabbit head for the nearest warren.

Not that I want to be getting myself dizzy finding my way in and out of a rabbit warren. I much prefer the two-roomed hutch I have, even if there are no mod cons!

One thing I'd like to know — why is it that whenever we rabbits hear you humans talking about our breeding, you have a pained look on your face? Some of us come from the best (and biggest) families!

OCCUPATIONAL HAZARDS
Two legged and four-legged poachers.
No family allowances.
The butcher, the baker, and fur-coat makers.

MOTTO
Lettuce be!

WHOEVER said "Man is the most intelligent species on earth" plainly didn't know what he was talking about.

Take this milk I'm trying to enjoy — only the lowest form of intelligence would ever design such a container for it. How can any self-respecting cat enjoy a dainty sip or two (or three or four) when one has to stick one's tongue down yards of narrow-necked bottle to get at the good stuff?

It's downright ridiculous, and you people should know better.

More proof — if more proof were needed — that you people are sadly lacking in top-quality brain power comes from the absolutely idiotic way in which good, rich, luscious catfood is sealed up in hard-to-open tins.

If the good Lord had meant us cats to eat out of tins, then cats would have had tin-openers on each paw, and not claws!

It's not so funny, either, the way you people tend to feed us cats on the "Have-you?" system. Don't pretend you don't know it!

"Have you fed the cat this morning?" says somebody.

"No. Haven't you?" says somebody else.

"No, I thought you had."

"Oh. Well, do you think — ?"

"H'm. I must say she looks hungry. She's eating pieces of coal."

"Give her something then. That cat is *always* hungry!"

And so on. Oh, don't think we cats don't listen to the things you say about us! And like elephants, we never forget.

I've got my own list of particular "Didn't-forget-who-said-it" items. I know perfectly well who said, "But I would rather have had a dog."

And I am well aware of the informer in our house who goes running to old You-Know-Who and says, "The cat's asleep on your bed again."

If only people realised that in this world we have all got to live and let live. We cats don't go around pushing dozing people off comfy armchairs before a blazing fire; we cats don't suddenly grab hold of people, lift them up, and stroke them furiously under their left ears; and we cats certainly would never dream of picking up people, taking them to the back door, and forcing them to go out into a cold, wet, windy night.

But people do all these things! You people really are a funny lot. Hard to understand, hard to live with, and hard by nature.

Not that I don't like people! Oh dear me, don't ever get that idea. I *love* people.

Which reminds me — do you happen to have a tin-opener on you? I could show you the catfood, you could open it, and I could eat it.

See what I mean about live and let live?

You lovely, darling, kind people! Of course you have your tin-opener with you . . .

MOTTO
Our bach is worse than our bite.

OCCUPATIONAL HAZARDS
Being kicked by Jones the Milk or Evans the Post.

Neglect on choir practice night.

Falling down old mine shafts.

Long-legged owners (even on short walks).

ONE thing about us Welsh Corgis, bach — we know our place. Even if some of us trot around at Royalty's heels, the rest of us are quite content to walk at somebody else's.

So if you haven't got a title or anything grand like that, don't feel you can't keep a Corgi.

You don't even have to be Welsh. We're democratic dogs, see. We like Scots, Irish and English. Mind you now — we love the Welsh. Who wouldn't?

It's been said of us that we're fat little things with no legs. We're not fat, see. We're stocky. And we have legs. Just try us, bach, when we get the scent of a Welsh harebit!

Do you like keeping up with the Joneses? Then you get yourself one of us, see. Then you'll be keeping up with every Taffy Jones (and a few thousand other people) in Wales.

And don't worry, see. We understand English.

WHOEVER said that human beings are the most intelligent of species was either a raving lunatic or a human being.

And that is my considered opinion . . . born of years of struggling to understand people.

Look at me — do I look as though I'm sitting here holding this stick in my mouth simply because I like the taste of it? Of course not!

I'm trying my darndest to tell that sprawling, lazy, slothful half-asleep bloke in the deck-chair that it's time he and I went out for some exercise.

I'm not doing myself any favours, you understand. He's the one who likes to go out most evenings about this time — before his favourite pub closes.

He won't admit to it, but I know I'm the best thing that ever happened to him. Until I came along he had a depressing time: he couldn't think up enough excuses for popping out for a quick one at his local.

Nowadays he rather tends to over-act. "Ah well." He sighs heavily. "I suppose I better take the dog out for his walk. Is it raining again?"

And with a glum face (he'll win himself an acting award one of these days) he starts to get ready while his wife fusses about him.

"See you're warmly wrapped up, dear," she says to him anxiously.

Nobody worries about whether I'm warmly wrapped up or not. Rain, ice, snow, fog or heatwave, I just have to go out the way I am.

"Walkies?" Ah, he's suddenly wakened up. Small wonder — the pub closes in 20 minutes time!

So we're off. Sixty yards down the road, 19 minutes sitting at his feet in the pub, and 60 yards back.

With only two lamp-posts within sight!

Why hasn't some human had the brains to design a pub with built-in lamp-posts?

Sometimes I feel so awfully frust-rated . . .

WE like people — especially people with stately homes and large bank accounts. People who can really afford us. Only the prlvlleged few, of course, for we Burmese cats are the upper-class aristocrats of feline society. We're rather rare, actually.

We have a position to maintain — although, admittedly, we get the occasional boorish urge to scrap with a Ginger Tom or a Tortoiseshell Tabby.

But most of the time we simply adore being fussed over and we always, but always, show our appreciation.

You won't find anyone of our breeding wasting our natural acting ability in advertising cat foods. Don't get me wrong though! We aren't snobs — good heavens no! We just like to mix with the right class and keep our social standing.

We like to grace the best homes — our etiquette is perfect and we are the most charming of cats. Do drop in for a sherry and meet us!

OCCUPATIONAL HAZARDS
Unfilleted salmon.
Yesterday's cream. We're very fastidious.
Our Siamese cousins.

MOTTO
Don't say cats,
say Burmese.

I DO like people. Honest I do. They're so good at opening milk bottles and tins of cat food. But possibly I like cats best. We're so intelligent, so clean and fastidious, so — well, let's face it, we're so superior. And of course many of us are pedigreed. Well, no, I'm not. But my mother, bless her sharp claws, knew a good Persian when she met him. It's true we're not so appreciative of people as we are of food, warmth and comfort. But just the same we can be very affectionate. We ask so little. Just a place to call our own in between hunting and exploring forays and, of course, some nice big gardens or fields in which to foray! If you don't have a cat try one of us. So dignified, so aloof, so quiet and relaxed. We don't ask much of anybody. Just their home . . .

OCCUPATIONAL HAZARDS
Milkmen going on strike.
Doors that won't open.
Owners who don't like dead mice.
Holiday-time for people.

MOTTO
Drinkapintamilkaday.

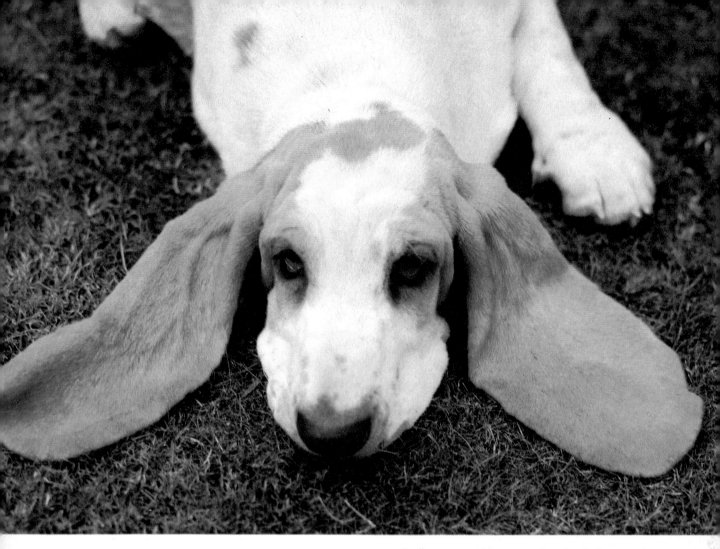

LET us start by talking about work. It is, if you must know, one of my favourite subjects.

Some of you people are far too fond of saying, "Hard work never harmed anyone." If I may say so, and I am going to say so, that view is not only a mistaken one, it is a downright dangerous diabolical one!

You people are so busy rushing from here to there, all in the name of work, that you simply don't have time to take note of the finer things of life.

Like warm sunshine to make you feel drowsy, and cool shade in which to avoid too much sun, and soft grass on which to lie.

Let us be honest with each other. When was the last time you lay snoozing in a shady spot? And I do it several times every day — !

Which brings me to my complaint against you people. It is quite clear that because you cannot personally enjoy shady spots in grassy places, you have embarked on a deliberate campaign to fill up every grassy area with concrete buildings, streets and pavements.

This is sheer cruelty, as you would know if you had the courage to lie on your tummy on burning-hot concrete. Don't believe me? Try it!

So can we reach agreement on a compromise?

Half the world's living area for you people to work away at, all industrious-like . . . and the other half to be left for me and my friends to lie upon . . .

Talking of lying around, have you people ever noticed how much noise a butterfly makes when passing by? It only takes two or three to flutter past, with an odd fly or two, and you'd think you were somewhere around a busy airport listening to heavy jet airliners!

Or the deafening howl of a breeze caressing the blades of grass? Or the heavy thump-thump of bees clumping around the pollen? Or the piercing shrieks of hysterical larks and cuckoos and all that noisy lot?

You'd think it wasn't asking too much of the world just to shut up for a spell and let a fella have a little shut-eye, would you?

Look, why don't you people just stop what you're doing, go out into the sunshine, lie down, close your ears and your eyes, and just gently drift off into a snooze?

Marvellous, isn't it? Try doing it more often!

MAYBE you're thinking of entering this gate? Well take my advice — and don't! Or I'll have you!

You heard right! I said I'll have you. I'm having one of my bad days, you see, so I'm not in the best of tempers.

All due to you people, of course.

You people, I'll have you know, have an outstanding talent for putting me in a bad mood. All because you people possess the most narrow-minded of outlooks and the most selfish of self-interests.

Take slippers, as a mere example. This world is full of slippers. Old slippers, new slippers, left-foot slippers, right-foot slippers. I could go on — and on — but I'm sure I've made my point.

So why the foaming at the mouth, the hysterical anger, the shouting of threats, simply because I happen to chew one old little-used slipper?

See what I mean? You people are the most unreasonable, illogical of creatures.

Take an important subject like food . . . If I happen to mention, with a polite bark or two, that I happen to be hungry — what happens?

You people, having stuffed yourselves silly with a three-four-five-six-course meal, look around in open irritation and glare at me.

"That beast hungry again? What's wrong with him? He was fed this morning . . . wasn't he?"

That's what you people say. Usually around seven o'clock in the evening.

So you will understand that, if you wish to stay fit and well, keep away from my gate. My motto for today is very definitely "They shall not pass."

Not, that is, unless they are bigger, faster, and more aggressive than me. So if you are about the size of a miniature Dachshund, as slow as a tortoise, and an arrant coward to boot, come on then, I'm ready for you. Oh, indeed, I'm spoiling for a fight with you.

But if you don't fit that description, see that you don't step on me as you barge past. That really would put me in a black mood.

Excuse me while I just practise my growls . . .

YOU people really are marvellous. I doff my beak to you. Why some of you can talk as well as us parrots. And most of you can squawk even louder.

It's a pity you're not clever enough to fly, or to sit contented for hours on a small stand in a wire cage.

And you're so generous with yourselves, too. Look at the way so many of you stick fingers through the wires of my cage just so I can have a big peck at them! (By the way, I do wish some of you would wash more often. A chap could catch germs pecking at dirty hands.)

Another little thing about you people is the way you stand up against my cage, press your face to the bars, and wait. What am I supposed to do? Turn somersaults? Do a song and dance?

And you're so eager to prove you can converse! But what's with all this "Pretty Polly" stuff? Is that how you people greet each other before you talk? I get tired of it I can tell you.

Maybe you think there's something odd about a colourful character like me stuck in a wire cage? Ugh! You should come to my place. We've got a little square box with people in it — and they talk so much I can't get a word in edgeways!

OCCUPATIONAL HAZARDS
Deaf people.
Cats who eat parrot-fashion.
The other squawk-box!
Pirates with bony shoulders!

MOTTO
Talk of the town.

HE really is a gorgeous gift to any cat with the brains to exploit him.

The day he arrived, I told him straight — "You're only allowed to stay if you and I get on."

That's the way it has to be, you know. Only one boss — and that's me. Mind you, I have my troubles with him. He still eats meat, chews bones and drinks water, despite my polite requests that he should demand fish, liver, and milk so that we can both enjoy his meals.

But he is very good at moving away smartly from the fire, giving up the best armchair, and growling ferociously at that snooty Siamese cat next door.

We have our fights, of course. He seems to have the oddest impulses to rebel, to assert himself, to do as he pleases.

But I must say a quick one-two with the paws, a good ear-splitting hiss, and a savage spit or two of fury gets him tame again.

Sometimes he says, "Why are you the boss around here when I'm so much bigger than you?"

"Ah yes," I say. "You're bigger, but I'm so much older than you. Look into my eyes," I say, "don't you see the wisdom and the knowledge that has been handed down through the centuries?"

And while he's looking, I bat him yet again with the old one-paw-two — and that ends that discussion for the time being.

He's not bad really. Mind you, he's not good! But he's not bad . . . not for a house-trained, cat-broken, half-starved, over-worked servant.

He's the only one I've got!

TAILPIECE
Whoever said "Let sleeping dogs lie" had no idea of what real fun can be.

OCCUPATIONAL HAZARDS		MOTTO
No other Siamese for miles around. Sore throats.	Satin bows. Cats that miaow.	'Cos Siam the best!

MEN who like to talk about motor cars (daft things!) talk in hushed whispers about a Rolls Royce or a Bentley. Well, please don't think I'm immodest, but we Siamese are the proverbial cat's whiskers in the cat world. We're expensive to buy. But isn't the best always expensive?

We're aloof, so people say, rarely show affection, and can be stubbornly independent. And extremely snooty. Don't you believe it!

Let me tell you the truth. It's all an act. A great big phony act.

Beneath our sleek, glossy, sable coats we're soft, friendly creatures. Really we are! If we like you, you're our friend for life. You can even eat some of our fish! But we don't seem to meet many people we like. Is that our fault?

Pardon me while I growl!

I CAN tell you, it's a tough life being an Alsatian. All this bally-hoo about us being the best, the fiercest, the most intelligent dogs in the canine world puts an awful burden on us, you know.

We're supposed to have film star looks. I blame old What's-his-name, Tin-Tin and-more-Tin or whatever it is, for all that malarkey. Every one of us Alsatians has it Rin-Tin-dinned into us how to sit, how to show our best profile, how to smile — "Always think of the cameras!" my mother used to say.

Being fierce — that puts a strain on. We're expected to face anything from a vicious gunman to a mob of rioters, and keep calm. Huh! Would you feel particularly calm facing the wrong end of a gun?

As for us being the most intelligent of dogs, well, I wouldn't exactly — er — disagree with that. But again, you see, it places such a burden, mentally speaking, on us.

I mean to say, where would all you good people be if the police forces didn't have us around? Law and order depends on us. So my old man once told me. And the country depends on law and order being upheld. So he said, and I wouldn't call him anything but truthful, the country depends on us.

I wonder if the Prime Minister and the rest of those politicians realise how much they owe to us?

OCCUPATIONAL HAZARDS
Cat-loving policemen.
Old films of Rin-Tin-Tin.
Small rooms.
Holiday-time kennels.

MOTTO
The K9 007.

I AM a most enthusiastic Do-It-Yourself fan. Oh yes, I'm dead keen on all that sort of jazz.

I've studied the subject, you know. After all, you can't do Do-It-Yourself if you don't know what you want to do.

I first got interested in the subject when I realised just how true it is that the good Lord helps those who help themselves. For nobody else was helping *me* to help myself to the good things, the really comfortable things, of life.

There and then I decided that if I wanted to get my claws on some tasty food, then I should not wait around merely hoping someone — anyone — would offer me a meal. I would henceforth Do-It-Myself.

I discovered that this meant that I ate when I wanted to — which is all the time I'm not sleeping.

Now there's another thing — the importance of *where* one sleeps. I don't suppose you people know what it's like to curl up for a good sleep on the floor?

It's hard, it's draughty, it's just plain uncomfortable — that's what it is.

But now that I'm in this Do-It-Myself lark, I sleep on armchairs, beds, settees — anywhere I fancy. I don't wait for someone to say, "Would you like to sleep on the cushions of the armchair?" Not me! I say it to myself, then accept the invitation.

That's what Do-It Yourself is all about.

And that's why I just don't understand all the fuss that's being made over some fish that's gone — er — missing. After all, I simply asked myself if I'd enjoy helping it off the plate and then accepted the invitation.

So I'd better make myself scarce for an hour or two until things quieten down. Other people can go all fanatical on this Do-It-Yourself, you know.

Like when it comes to handing out a little punishment, they're so keen to Do-It-Themselves.

Oh dear, I think I'm going to have indigestion just at the thought . . .

W E certainly do like people. Mind you, we're not so sure we like the way people live. Frankly, we are bewildered and bemused at some of the things people do!

Take the way people eat, for example. So much fuss and hard work to produce a simple meal! Masses of kettles, saucepans, dishes and cutlery — all to be got out, and then put away.

We like our way best. A simple saucer well filled . . . and we leave it as clean as a whistle.

Take the way people design their homes, as another example. All these doors and windows that shut you off from the good fresh air! It is very frustrating, you know, to have to sit patiently at a closed door or window, hoping someone will come along and let us out.

Pardon us for saying so, but we think people are rather selfish. On cold nights when everybody wants near the fire, who always gets the best positions? Not us!

And we like armchairs, too, you know. So why this strange human custom only buying one for each side of the fireside . . . and throwing us off when we try to use them?

We could go on and on . . . but perhaps you'd get the wrong idea and think we don't like people!

We do, we do! We believe wholeheartedly that all cats should have people around . . . to open doors, windows, catfood tins, milk bottles — and their hearts!

OCCUPATIONAL HAZARDS
Dog lovers.
Middle-of-the-night serenaders.

MOTTO
Purry-ty good.

OH, my aching head! I do wish that fly on the other side of the room would stop making such an infernal, deafening racket!

Boy, did I have a ball last night! So all right, I did have a bone or two more than I should have done, to say nothing of a little too much gravy and milk (oh, did I mix my drinks! I'll say!).

It was my party, and I had all the gang in. Everybody brought a friend . . . though I still want to find out who was so stupid as to bring that great lump of a St Bernard. The way she downed bones was just nobody's business. That girl has real problems: she's all weight and no waste, if you get what I mean.

But the highlight of the evening was the sing-song we had. It was marvellous — all 14 of us barking so beautifully as we rendered "Down By The Old Mill Stream."

Old You-Know-Who was visibly moved by the song. I can vouch for that, for he moved out of his bed, shot down the stairs, and charged up to us just as we finished.

"Don't ever let me hear that again," he said . . . and I saw tears in his eyes.

I would never have thought Old You-Know-Who was the emotional type.

The party got a bit wild after he'd gone. We played "Hunt The Slipper" and "Postman's Knock." The slippers were rather badly chewed, I'm afraid, and as we didn't have a real postman, we simply had to make do with some ancient trousers of Old You-Know-Who and rip them to pieces.

But let's face it — I don't go much on these mornings-after! Oh, my aching head!

And by the time I've cleared up the bits of bones, lifted all the empty milk bottles, rolled the carpet back, and hidden all the chewed slippers, it's going to be a case of "Oh, my aching back!"

Party? Did you say anything about a party? Well, it so happens that there's nothing better for a hangover than the hair of the human and all that . . . and I'm not doing anything tonight . . .

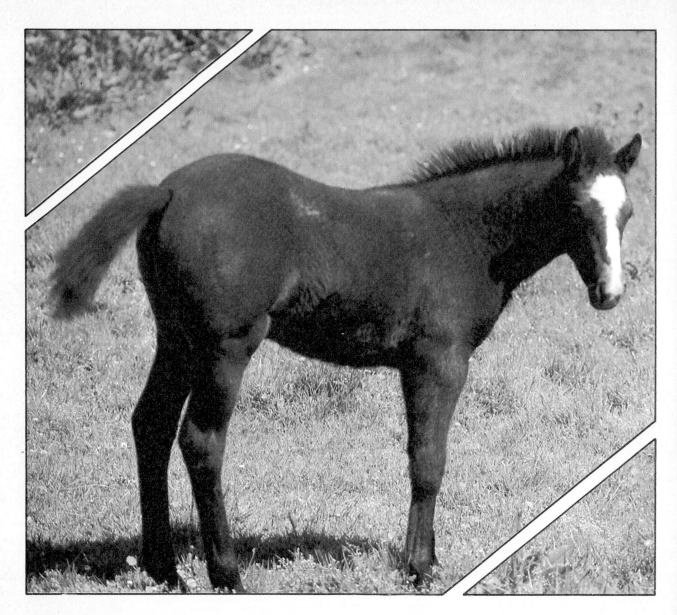

HONESTLY, I'm not going to say a word against cats or dogs. Mind you, I'm not going to say much for them either.

But if you care to think for a moment about which animal has the most charm, grace, intelligence, strength, loyalty, to say nothing of usefulness — well, what other answer can you give but . . . a horse!

Of course, there are some minor snags about keeping a horse as a pet. Like having a field to keep it in (if you're really horsey-minded you call it a paddock and impress your friends), bales of hay to keep it chewing happily, and a little time and lots of energy in keeping it clean and healthy.

But in return you have yourself a steed that will carry you with the speed of light wherever you want to go.

If you don't really fancy a gallop into the setting sun, you can have a trot along the skyline, or an amble into the heat of the day.

You'll notice how lyrical we horses are. That's because we're creatures of artistic temperament — sensitive, lovable.

As you'll be . . . if you're ever lucky enough to own such a noble friend as a horse! That's honest — straight from a horse's mouth.

OCCUPATIONAL HAZARDS

Mechanical Transport.
Saddles.
Cobbled streets.
Sugar not in lumps.
TV Cowboys.

MOTTO

One Horsepower — unlimited miles per gallop.

O F course I've heard of Bigheads, but this is plain ridiculous! I don't know why they ever bought him in the first place. After all, who needs a dog the size of a half-grown elephant?

All he ever does is eat and sleep. And when it comes to eating — oh crikey! You should hear him slop-slurp-slap at his food!

He's the world's best sleeper. He sleeps at any time, any place, in any weather. I wouldn't mind so much if only he would stop coming to sleep beside me.

"More matey like," he says, and crashes to the floor like a demolished building . . . and then begins to snore, scratch, twitch, heave and grunt. It's unbelievable!

Seven of my nine lives have been used up already with him having nightmares.

But he means well, you know. And he can be useful. Like washing me all over in two licks. Like keeping out draughts. Like reaching food from off the kitchen table. Like keeping other cats out of our garden.

And he's got such a beautiful nose on which to dab a sharp claw just once in a while . . .

TAILPIECE

Whoever said, "Good things come in small doses," could only have been a cat lover.

OCCUPATIONAL HAZARDS
Unco-operative butchers.
Cat lovers.
Houseproud housewives.
Unsnobbish people.

MOTTO
We nose, you know.

I DO, I really, really do like people. But the trouble is, you see, I'm a snob. An out-and-out one hundred per cent. snob!

Oh, I know I look an adorable puppy. I am. Very adorable! But young as I am, I look for — I demand — the best that's going.

(By the way, don't call me "cute little fella" — please. I don't want any trouble, but I hate being called "cute" or "little" or even "fella." If you don't mind? Thank you.)

Well, as I was saying, a Beagle expects the best. You don't see a Beagle running along behind an owner who can only afford a push-bike. (Oh dear, the very thought makes me shudder!) But you will see us getting in and out of Rolls Royces, Bentleys, Mercedes and even — if we must — some of these estate cars that have special compartments for us dogs.

We get our pictures in all the best society magazines, for we belong to the huntin', shootin', fishin' types. The open-air sportsmen. Take us out to the countryside, turn us loose, and before you can say, "Seek 'em!" we'll show you how a real dog gets to work . . .

Now if you're one of these strangely fussy types who, for quaint personal reasons, objects to scratches on newly-painted doors or silly old polished pieces of furniture, I warn you (in the friendliest manner) that I like scratching doors and pieces of furniture.

I also like digging up lawns, frightening postmen with a really loud "Grrr!" (I wouldn't really bite! They taste so — ugh!)

I also chew slippers, newspapers and magazines you haven't had time to read, and (though I don't really mean to) tear nylons.

Just look at me — did you ever see such a ferocious devil like me? Ah, I'm a wild 'un, I tell you!

And that's nothing! Wait till I grow up!

Now, now, now — don't be too hasty! That's the trouble with you humans. You're so darned impulsive. So I'm a snob, so I happen to have a little weakness or two . . . that's no reason to start thinking about buying yourself some meek, mild, unimaginative breed!

Didn't I tell you — I like people. I'd like YOU.

Needing a dog? Then you need a Beagle. You need me. 'Cos I need you!

WE cats are supposed to be domestic tigers who stalk birds or mice or ambush over-inquisitive dogs. Well, I'm not like that.

I like comfort. I like my basket (placed near a warm fire, thank you), and the very thought of going out into the cold, wet open-air to stalk hoppity birds and scuttling mice just makes me feel limp!

As for dogs — as long as one doesn't lie in my basket, drink off my milk saucer, or touch my fish . . . why should I cause any trouble?

It's so nice and peaceful just to lie around, give myself a lick or two, stretch now and again (I have to go outside some time or other for a couple of minutes) and then go back to sleep.

And this life of mine, this gentle idyll of grow-fatter-by-the-day, and lazier-by-the-week, comes to me from people.

Wonderful, generous, milk-supplying, food-producing people.

Do I like people?

I LOVE 'EM!

OCCUPATIONAL HAZARDS
Draughts.
Small baskets.
Overweight.
Insomnia.

MOTTO
Let sleeping cats lie.

I DON'T feel so good at the moment. I feel a little peaky, if you know what I mean. That's why I'm resting.

I think it is rather nice of you lot to have such charming snoozing baskets made especially for the likes of me. And don't think I'm not truly appreciative merely because I would like to suggest that a little more padding and an electric blanket would be most welcome.

I trust you won't get annoyed at me if I continue with a subject so close to my purring heart.

Cats, being truly superior, need all the exquisite comfort, all the rich indolent luxury, and all the elegant trappings that you lot can continue to produce. It's not asking much, is it?

After all, darn it, we cats don't ask much more from you than somewhere to eat, and the odd gallon or two to drink.

Well, having said my little piece, I think I'll go on guard duty, that is to say, that though my eyes will be shut, and my head might sink to my paws, and my tail will be curled around to keep out draughts, I shall actually be ALERT and AT THE READY.

Just let anything — be it Martian or human or any other kind of monster — come barging in round here, and I shall have him!

That's the way I work. Always on the go, I am. If I were to tell you just how great I really am, your head would simply reel, really it would.

I do wish you'd stop laughing at me. You'll only get a stitch in your side . . .

Let me say right away, ladies, I'm English through and through. Honestly, I don't know what people who buy pets can be thinking of putting foreigners like West Highland terriers (get a haircut, Mac!), Burmese cats (who speaks Burmese anyway?) and Welsh Corgis before a home breed like me! We Bulldogs are about as English as village greens, pubs with thatched roofs, roast beef, and all that. You won't find a better house dog anywhere! I admit, because I'm a modest, honest chap, that we can't wash and dry dishes, or cook really super Yorkshire puddings. But just let anyone take the slightest liberty with you or yours — and we'll have him! Oh, yes, we'll have him! That's us, ladies, devoted to those we love.

And don't make the mistake that big dogs make, of judging us by our size. Maybe we are a little on the small side, but we're big hearted. And scared of nothing!

OCCUPATIONAL HAZARDS
Never being challenged
to a fight.
Cat lovers.

MOTTO
Don't push me!

THE trouble with people is — they are fussy! So drive-you-round-the-bend fussy!

They fuss about where they sit, they fuss about the weather, they fuss about their food, they fuss about the company they keep, they fuss about what's on TV, and they even fuss about what they are going to do to fill in their leisure hours.

Oh believe me, you people don't half *fuss!*

Now far be it from me to go around boasting about how much more intelligent we cats are (and after all, *everybody* but *everybody* knows we are!) but I will say that we cats never fuss.

You can call us Pussy if you must; but you can never call us Fussy.

No matter what happens, we take life calmly, unblinkingly, equably. We are always dignified, gracious and understanding.

We are also, in addition to being surprisingly modest, most undemanding.

Give us frequent platefuls of good wholesome nosh such as fish or liver, pints of extra-creamy milk, a not-too-Spartan spot on which to rest our weary bodies — such as a silk cushion, a cosy armchair, or a switched-on electric blanket, and lots and lots of undisturbed peace . . . and we're satisfied.

It's leading such simple, uncomplicated lives that makes us the popular, undemanding, lovable creatures that we are!

But you people — ! Our hearts bleed for you. We feel for you. We really would like to help you, believe me.

But there is a SNAG. (Isn't there always?)

There are limited supplies of good nosh and extra-creamy milk so frankly we would prefer you people to stick to your tripe and onions and your cups of tea.

Also, and more important, there is already a world shortage of cosy resting places in which to snooze, so I see little point in encouraging you people to curl up for the best part of each day.

Don't think I'm being selfish. Only practical! Be honest — can you people see yourselves enjoying a layabout's existence in a basket like the one I'm occupying? You see what I mean? You people are not only wrong in the way you live, you people are all wrong, in size and height and inclination, to change to any other way.

So I'm afraid you people will just have to carry on doing all your household chores, or battling out into the rain and snow and fog for shopping, or washing those endless piles of clothes which you will insist on wearing.

Oh how my poor heart bleeds for you. One last point — do your work quietly, *please?* I'm about to take a well-earned snooze . . .

NOW just for starters, please cut out the usual "Look out — there's Supersonic flashing past!" or the other usual "Hey — don't you know there's a speed limit around here?"

Too many of you lot spend most of your time rushing around all busy-busy — and for what? So that you can sink into a cosy armchair, limp and exhausted, and wail, "Oh what a day I've had!"

Us tortoises live to very ripe old ages. And that's because we never hurry. We go slow; we often stop to have a long, long think before we hide away for an even longer, longer sleep (hibernation, I believe you lot call it — wot big words you do use!).

Now some of you lot — who must surely be myopic — say we are not good looking. Others dare to say that as pets we are really useless.

All lies put out by them wot pride themselves on great hulking pets who chase after balls and sticks to retrieve them — just so they can be thrown away again.

Of course we are good looking . . . ask any female tortoise. Of course we are useful — lawn-cropping, lettuce-thinning, food-scrap disposal, to name but a few.

But we do NOT like to be considered attractive and useful as tortoiseshell covers for compacts, ciggy boxes, combs, etc., etc. and etc.

Affectionate? Of course we are. Take us into your warm bed, and we'll stay there for six months!

You do have an electric blanket — then wot are we waiting for . . . ?

LIFE gets so tedious, don't it? Ho-hum, it's a *very tiring* business lolling around here most of the day doing nothing. I get so exhausted with yawning and so worn out with snoozing! I shall have to take some sort of tonic to keep up with my sleep.

Mind you, appearances can be most deceptive. Just because I lie around here looking casually bored, don't think I'm wasting time. There are probably lots of things I'm very busy *thinking* about.

Just so as you will appreciate what a strenuous life I lead just in thinking alone, I'll tell you what I'm thinking about right now. I've been thinking about how much more comfortable this residence of mine would be if I had a lovely soft cosy cushion on which I could recline. I've been thinking of all the possible places from which I could beg, borrow or steal such a lovely cushion.

And I have been thinking how much simpler and less exhausting it would be if someone — like yourself, for example — would go and get it for me.

These are but a few of the profound thoughts that rush around inside my brain. I won't even mention to you how often I think about such serious matters as fish, fish and more fish . . . or even of saucers, pails, and vats of milk.

But I have spent a little time thinking about what I shall do for today. And I have come to a decision.

Today I shall be a MONSTER.

As you can see, I am already playing my part. I look ferocious, mean, evil, even loathsome. As a MONSTER, there's no doubt that I am a terrifying blood-curdling success.

Of course I shall actually have to terrify, to blood-curdle, someone . . . and I know just the right subject. That silly tortoise will try to flash past me at his usual jet-propelled speed . . . and at the right moment, I shall *snarl*.

Oh, I shall have fun being a real horrible MONSTER!

On the other hand, now I come to think some more about it, it does seem an awful lot of hard work — snarling and all that.

Perhaps I'm being a little hasty in being a MONSTER today, when I could be a Larder Robber instead — and with much more reward to show for my efforts.

Liver and kidneys delivered only this morning. I smelled 'em! And they are in that larder somewhere . . .

Heigh-ho . . . seventeen paces to the larder, seventeen paces back, lots and lots of munching (in a hurry, too!) — oh dear, life simply is very tedious.

THOUGH I like people, the odd thing is, so few people like me.

All right, all right, so I don't exactly look like an advertisement for toothpaste. A chap can't help his looks!

Besides, we Bloodhounds have a lot to be fed up about. Look at the way you people avoid us!

Would *you* have a Bloodhound for a pet? Of course you wouldn't. Do you know anyone who would? 'Course you don't! You think of us only as howling our heads off at the end of a chain as we tear in pursuit of fugitives or convicts.

Actually we only do it because it's expected of us. We're really such friendly, lovable creatures.

We like to play just like other dogs. We're intelligent, charming, handsome — in a dignified sort of way — and very loyal.

What more could anyone ask for in a pet?

You — you wouldn't like to have me? No, I thought not.

It's a cat's life!

OCCUPATIONAL HAZARDS
Skinned noses.
Colds in the head.
People who walk in rivers.
My name: "Bloodhound" — I ask you!
Muddy countryside.

MOTTO
Heaven-scent!

I HAVE always thought he was a drip. All dogs are, you know. But lately he's become such a *wet* drip.

Frankly I think he's gone round the bend. He's obsessed with water. His favourite quotation seems to be "Water, water, everywhere — and all of it to wash in."

He's such a crazy fool that he actually goes around begging, in that sickening barking way of his, for his bath to be filled so that he can dive in and splash.

Ugh!

Then of course we have the revolting ritual of scented soaps and perfumed shampoos. Really, it makes a cat wonder what dogs are coming to these days!

But what really chills my spine, what really makes my fur rise in hackled fury, is when the silly goof looks at me and says why don't you come in and join me?

I give myself another one or two fastidious licks just to ensure I'm shining clean, and then look at him in disgust.

Go ahead, I say, risk drowning if you must. Eat soap lather if you want to. Flirt with pneumonia if you feel reckless.

But leave me and my nine lives alone!

Oh dear — there goes the kitchen tap. That means he'll be getting off this chair and . . .

I think I'll go under the sideboard for the next 10 minutes . . .

TAILPIECE
Whoever said "Cleanliness is next to godliness" could only have owned a cat.

THERE I was padding along a wall, minding my own business (which is to look out for field mice and non-flying birds) when this bloke stops me and says, ''Hi, beautiful! I'll bet a good-looking cat like you is already under contract to some Hollywood photographer.''

Well, I know at once from the description to whom he is talking, so I stop. It so happens that I am not, at the moment, under contract to any photographer, Hollywood or otherwise. And in my own way, such as jumping down from the wall and stalking round his trouser leg all stiff-tailed, I let him know.

The upshot is that he simply raves over me, particularly once I show him my best profile.

''I'll make you famous!'' he cries. ''Come wiz me, darleeng, to my studio.''

Let's be honest — I would prefer he lure me to a fish cannery or a petfood factory or a super-sized dairy. But let's not get too studious about mere studios . . .

Besides, I already see myself — the Lassie of the cat world — stalking silently, lithely, through the savage jungle of London as I save you people once again from Martian invaders or foreign tourists or the blare of the Karri-Cassette Gangs . . .

So I go to his studio, and pose daintily while he scurries around putting on lights and what have you. Clearly, he is afraid to be in the dark with me. This boy knows a tiger when he sees me!

I am wondering whether I should suggest diving through an eight-inch circle of fire from a height of 70 feet . . . or swimming under the surface in a 20-foot deep vat of milk (oh, what a glorious way to go!) when he gives me this odd mean look.

''In here!'' he says — and dumps me (and I've got dignity like everybody else!) in this — this thing!

You could bowl me over, I tell you!

What about the action then, I wonder. Where's the dashing female I'm supposed to rescue? Where's the rest of you people I'm supposed to save? Where's the epic drama so necessary to a dynamic clean-cut-all-action star like me?

''You wot?'' he says brutally. ''Sit there, shut up, and watch for the birdie!''

Lucky for him he says a word like ''birdie.'' I sit, waiting hopefully as you can see.

The photo fella went home hours ago. But me — I'm still waiting and watching.

That birdie can't hide for ever . . .

WHOEVER said "Sticks and stones may break my bones but names will never hurt me" was certainly not a cat. Which means they were not very intelligent.

On behalf of all cats everywhere, I stand here to address you lot as a form of protest.

I protest against the staggering lack of tact and imagination which is consistently shown by you lot to us lot on the question of our names.

Just think about it! Look at the usual choice — "Pooh," "Blackie," "Fishface," "Sissy," "Ginger," and so on and so on until one feels close to choking with disgust.

Is that really the best we can expect? The limit of your low, exhausted imaginations? Do me a favour!

Look at me — look at your own cat. And ask yourself if the name you have chosen is suitably apt for so noble a creature. Does the name bestowed have a touch of dignity, a ring of aristocracy, a weight of intelligence, a quintessence of uniqueness?

Care to bet on the answers?

I have never been known to answer to it, but I am called "Squiff," or as some even say it, "Squiffey." Charming!

I have therefore decided, and I announce it now once and for all time, that my name from now on shall be Algy Archibald, Earl of The Alley, and I will only answer to that . . . and to the sounds of my food plate being filled.

Cats of the world unite — and refuse to answer to yelps and cries of "Pusspuss — here, pretty pusspuss!"

If you can't choose a name, choose a number. Make it a swinging one!

As we cats say, you only live nine times, you know!

YOU can stop grinning for a start. Haven't you ever seen talent before?

I had no intention of taking up a musical career. My thoughts were on a higher plane — like the study of bones, the researching of butchers' shops and the pursuit of postmen.

But old You-Know-Who struck at me in a vicious, hurtful, underhanded way just the other day.

He was watching as I dutifully polished off a huge plateful of food. Then he glared at me. Yes, glared!

"You know what you are, don't you?" he snarled at me, nearly giving me indigestion as I bolted my nosh. "You're a parasite, that's what! You never do anything for yourself!".

Well! How rude can human beings be? After me being prepared to dedicate my life to eating his food, sharing his home, enjoying his garden (to say nothing about guarding him from that fierce brute of a kitten next door) — that's the thanks I get!

Right, I said. OK, I said. Now I know, I said. If I'm not welcome here . . .

I'm going to make my own way in the world. As the best dog-pianist act anywhere, I'll earn huge sums of lolly and set up my own dog-food factory and chain of butchers' shops — to say nothing of buying whole streets and streets of lamp-posts just for my own use.

But of course it takes years and years and years (if not longer) to train as a musician (you don't think I chose such a career by accident, do you? Give me credit!).

So, in the meantime, I'm staying on with old You-Know-Who, eating his food, sharing his — well, and all that jazz. It's a sacrifice, but I'm willing.

Besides, the look of pain on his face when I scamper up and down the piano keyboard makes it all worth while. Sort of strikes the right note — for me!

YOU know, it's a hard life being so good looking as I am. The times I spend under the hot studio lights posing for batteries of cameras — all right, all right, the odd camera, since you insist! — always preening myself, always rippling the odd feather or two, and even giving vent to whistling such wonderful songs as "You must have been a beautiful egg, baby, for baby, look at you now."

Of course being a top model has its dangers. For example, I notice cats are awfully keen to end my dazzling career. Jealousy, sheer utter jealousy, I suppose.

Then there's you lot. For reasons unknown to me, you want me to make speeches. Oh, not the long boring ones you lot make to each other! More short important announcements like "Ten minutes till the pubs shut," or "Give us a kiss, love!" or even "Doing anything tonight, darling?"

Old You-Know-Who is always teaching me things like that so that I can converse with you lot. There's so many he's taught me, but I can't tell you all of them because She-Who-Is-Boss yells at me when I repeat them.

I learned of her disapproval when the vicar called one day, and I spoke to him, chummy like, in words I'd learned from You-Know-Who.

Mind you, the row I got was a gentle reproof compared to the earful he got when he breezed in at tea-time!

Oh well, time to go to work. Quick look in the mirror to make sure I'm as exquisitely beautiful as ever, look the camera straight in its eye, say to myself "Watch the mannie now!" — and there's another masterpiece on film!

Who's a pretty boy then?

I am, I am, I am!